PAUSE FO

Word Searches
for
Tranquility

Eric & Janinne Berlin

PUZZLE
WRIGHT
PRESS

New York

PUZZLE
WRIGHT
PRESS

New York

PUZZLEWRIGHT PRESS and the distinctive Puzzlewright Press logo
are registered trademarks of Sterling Publishing Co., Inc.

ISBN 978-1-4549-5029-5

For information about custom editions, special sales, and premium purchases,
please contact specialsales@unionsquareandco.com.

Manufactured in Canada

2   4   6   8   10   9   7   5   3   1

unionsquareandco.com

Cover design by Elizabeth Mihaltse Lindy
Cover image by Bibadash/Shutterstock.com

CONTENTS

INTRODUCTION

Welcome to "Pause for Puzzles: Word Searches for Tranquility"! A few puzzles within these pages have very tranquil themes, including yoga, hobbies, and crafts. But honestly, we find just about any word search can be a source of tranquility. A word search engages the mind, of course, like any puzzle does … but not to an intense degree. These aren't super-hard sudoku; these aren't difficult crosswords with a lot of tricky vocabulary. You know right up front: You're not going to get stuck on any of these puzzles, and you're not going to find yourself frustrated (at least, not for terribly long). All you need to do is sit back, relax, and enjoy.

Odds are you don't need instructions for these puzzles, but just to be on the safe side: Each grid of letters hides a number of words and phrases—always in a straight line going up, down, left, right, or diagonally—ignoring any spaces, punctuation, or accent marks. Words will overlap each other, so don't blot out letters as they're used; they might get used again. When you've found every word in the puzzle, read the leftover letters row by row for a quote or message related to that puzzle's theme.

We enjoyed making these puzzles for you, and we hope you get a lot of enjoyment and relaxation out of solving them!

—Eric & Janinne Berlin

You Earned It

ACCLAIM

ACCOLADES

APPLAUSE

APPRECIATION

AWARD

BLUE RIBBON

CHAMPIONSHIP

COMPENSATION

CONGRATULATIONS

CROWN

DISTINCTION

FAME

GLORY

GOLD WATCH

HIGH FIVE

HONOR

KUDOS

LAURELS

MERIT BADGE

PAT ON THE BACK

PRIZE

RAISE

RAVE REVIEW

RENOWN

SCHOLARSHIP

TROPHY

```
W E I V E R E V A R G R E A
T G P J O Z E S U A L P P A
B D S I I G O L D W A T C H
K A O R H Y L V I T N N G T
U B P H H S I S O H O N O R
D T S P W O N N R B D N S E
O I O A A R T O B C O D H N
S R S W C H E I I I M R E O
T E A T E C R T T P N A H I
I M T B I E O A W E M W I T
R E A S U N S L U P E A G A
S C R L P N C U A R O L H I
K L B U E D A T O D O F F C
Y O E P U C L A I R E E I E
T S M R C G R R Y O O S V R
S O O L U A L G V E N A E P
C N A O I A T N W O N E R P
P I H S R A L O H C S H E A
M R E M A F O C R O W N N E
```

Answer on page 104.

A Day at the Beach

BATHING SUIT

BIKINI

BOARDWALK

BOAT

CATAMARAN

COOLER

CORAL

FRISBEE

HERMIT CRAB

JELLYFISH

KAYAK

LIFEGUARD

LOW TIDE

OCEAN

PARASAILING

SALT WATER

SANDCASTLE

SAND DUNE

SCUBA

SEAGULL

SEAWEED

SHELLS

SHORELINE

SNORKEL

SPLASH

SURFBOARD

SWIMMING

VOLLEYBALL

WAVES

WHARF

```
R T H E P E N U D D N A S H
E E I C A T A M A R A N N S
E E L T S A C D N A S K S A
B B A O C E A N S O N D B L
S O A E O A C A A B U C S P
I A H R I C L N T F H E A S
R T B A C T H A H R M R A I
F R A H W T S S I U A S N P
I N B A T H I N G S U I T D
L K T D V F U M A E K T R E
A E O T Y O H I R I E A S E
R H E L L L L S B E U O K W
O S L F M I I I C G H R A A
C E O S N O R K E L S V Y E
J A C G O P I F C Y E C A S
O G N I M M I W S S B R K A
L U E N I L E R O H S A I N
K L A W D R A O B S E C L T
S L L E H S S E D I T W O L
```

Answer on page 104.

Ice Cream Shop

BLENDER

BUTTERSCOTCH

CARAMEL

CHOCOLATE

COFFEE

COOKIE DOUGH

FREEZER

FROZEN YOGURT

FRUIT SMOOTHIE

FUDGE SWIRL

GELATO

HAND-PACKED PINT

HOT FUDGE

MILKSHAKE

ROOT BEER FLOAT

SCOOP

SHERBET

SOFT SERVE

STRAWBERRY

SUNDAE

SYRUP

TORTE

VANILLA

WAFFLE CONE

WHIPPED CREAM

```
I Y R R E B W A R T S T W A
W S N T P R C B L E N D E R
E H C E T R O T A L E G E I
S E I L Y I O C E C I G R E
T N I P D E K C A P D N A H
S Y R U P A I M B U U T A A
T L R E Z E E R F E X A N V
D A E R T H D T E B R E H S
E E O G E N O C E L F F A W
R A E L A H U T R U E N J E
E O D Y F E G D D E S N O T
K W F N L R H G A V A O R A
A E D W U I E C A R A M E L
H C T O C S R E T T U B T O
S H H O W N E Y B A N D P C
K N E I E V R E S T F O S O
L T R U G O Y N E Z O R F H
I L C T E E F F O C A O R C
M E I H T O O M S T I U R F
```

Answer on page 105.

Knitting and Crafts

APPLIQUÉ

BASTING

BUTTONHOLE

CROSS-STITCH

DOUBLE CROCHET

DRAPE

EMBROIDERY

HOOP

INTERFACING

LACE

LINING

NEEDLEPOINT

NOTIONS

PATCHWORK

PATTERNS

PLEATS

QUILT

RUFFLE

SCRAPS

SEWING

SKEIN

SLIPKNOT

SPINNING

TASSEL

TATTING

THIMBLE

THREAD

WEFT

WOOL

YARDAGE

YARN

ZIGZAG

```
S  W  H  L  P  A  S  T  A  E  L  P  T  E
K  E  N  I  O  N  G  L  S  P  A  R  C  S
E  L  W  N  O  I  G  N  I  T  S  A  B  E
I  S  H  I  H  I  D  I  C  P  G  O  M  P
N  T  T  N  N  H  O  H  U  N  K  G  H  A
T  O  T  G  O  G  W  H  I  B  E  N  I  R
N  T  E  H  C  O  R  C  E  L  B  U  O  D
N  S  C  P  R  I  A  T  R  R  O  E  D  T
E  B  A  K  Y  F  S  I  E  U  W  O  E  N
T  L  L  N  R  A  Y  T  G  I  F  L  W  I
A  N  B  E  G  Z  T  S  N  T  O  F  A  O
T  N  T  M  I  L  N  S  I  H  D  C  L  P
T  N  L  G  I  R  O  S  N  R  T  E  H  E
I  E  Z  U  E  H  S  O  N  E  M  G  T  L
N  A  Q  T  A  K  T  R  I  A  I  A  F  D
G  N  T  G  M  T  E  C  P  D  S  D  E  E
A  A  N  S  U  E  V  E  S  S  R  R  W  E
P  E  M  B  R  O  I  D  E  R  Y  A  Y  N
T  H  I  E  U  Q  I  L  P  P  A  Y  N  G
```

Answer on page 105.

Under the Sea

ANEMONE

BARRACUDA

BLUE MARLIN

CARP

CONCH

CORAL REEF

DOLPHIN

ELECTRIC EEL

FLOUNDER

GIANT CLAM

GUPPY

HUMPBACK WHALE

KELP

MUDSKIPPER

NARWHAL

OCTOPUS

ORANGE ROUGHY

ORCA

PERCH

PORPOISE

SARDINE

SEA CUCUMBER

SHRIMP

SOLE

STINGRAY

STURGEON

TILAPIA

```
E E L O S L F E C O T R Y I
R N C M E T E L C L S P H C
G E I A U N I T O S P T G H
U I B H N D O N T U H E U L
I R A M P P S P G R N M O A
A E C N U L Y K B R P D R H
U C A S T C O T I B A T E W
B A R R A C U D A P H Y G R
L E P O O Y L C A L P L N A
U S O N U S K A A E E E A N
F T C H T W S E M E I R R E
M H L E H I C T C T S P O R
A I S A C A L I U L O S I E
R G L A C O R A L R E E F N
L E N A R T L L P I G P K O
I E R A C D D O A I R E T M
N O H E P M I R H S A R O E
E L L P T S H N E M N C A N
V E I G E A P L E K T H E A
```

Answer on page 106.

Art Is Everywhere

À LA CARTE

APARTMENT

ARTICHOKE HEART

ARTIFACT

BONAPARTE

CLEAR THE AIR

DARTMOUTH

DEPARTMENT

GO-KART

IMPARTIAL

MAGNA CARTA

MARTHA STEWART

MARTIN

MOTHER EARTH

PAR THREE

PARTITION

PARTY HEARTY

QUARTERS

REPARTEE

SMART START

SPARE PARTS

SPARTAN

STAR TREK

TARTAN

TARTAR SAUCE

WORRYWART

```
A T R A C A N G A M M R A T
D R N U E A R S O A T E I T
S E T E I S P N R K O P R R
T O P N M A E T W H A A O A
I M P A R T I A L I E R S T
I M N T R N R S P H T T T S
R I A F H T R A E L C E I T
H N R R E D M K P P A E B R
T M U T T O O E N A F S E A
U E O W H H O I N R I T C M
O P N T C S A S P T T R U S
M I A I H R R S E H R A A A
T Y T R A E H Y T R A P S L
R R S S T A R T R E K E R A
A O T R H I A E E E W R A C
D R A S S R T A A L V A T A
A U D O T R D I A R L P R R
Q T R A W Y R R O W T S A T
B O N A P A R T E N I H T E
```

Answer on page 106.

Motown Hits

ALL NIGHT LONG

BABY LOVE

BERNADETTE

BRICK HOUSE

CLOUD NINE

COME SEE ABOUT ME

CRUISIN'

EASY

FOR ONCE IN MY LIFE

GET READY

IT TAKES TWO

LET IT WHIP

LET'S GET IT ON

LOVE CHILD

MY CHERIE AMOUR

MY GUY

NIGHTSHIFT

PLEASE MR. POSTMAN

SHOP AROUND

SIR DUKE

STILL

THESE EYES

```
E T T E D A N R E B D L O Y
M O A L L N I G H T L O N G
U Y K N I O E W W I S H I C
N C C H H O K F T T E H O E
A C S H C E U S G R Y M E E
M L S A E T D S O N E G S F
T O P H V R R E R S E F O I
S U R N O T I T E G S T E L
O D M E L P S E D B E Y I Y
P N P M T H A E A M H T Y M
R I I Y A B R R V M T E D N
M N H G O L A E O A O T A I
E E W U H T N B K U E U C C
S S T Y W T I E Y A N S R C
A M I M E A S Y O L T D T N
E O T W N T I H S F O I E O
L R E S W T U N I U M V G R
P B L O E R R O N F E H E O
E S U O H K C I R B T I T F
```

Answer on page 107.

Let's Make a Movie

ACADEMY AWARD

ACTOR

BEST PICTURE

CAMERA

CELEBRITIES

CLASSICS

COMPOSER

DOCUMENTARY

DRAMA

EDITOR

EXTRA

GENRE

LINES

NOMINATION

PREVIEW

PRODUCER

PROP

RED CARPET

SCENE

SILVER SCREEN

SOUNDSTAGE

STUDIO

STUNT

TALKIES

THEATER

THEME MUSIC

WORLD PREMIERE

WRITER

```
S E I K L A T O E N E C S S
E T H E M E M U S I C T C E
I A U Y R A T N E M U C O D
T R W D I U N N I N N G R I
I E P D I I T R T E C A T T
R G R O R O T C A R W S H O
B A E E T E V E I A N E S R
E T V A I O N D Y P A E L R
L S I R B M E M E T T R I G
E D E E E H E P E F I S N L
C N W M M D R R R E R N E G
E U D A A O C E P A X C S B
O O U C D P S A L D E T O F
A S A U H O R I R S L M R O
M S C T P E E R E P C R E A
A E N M T T V M O P E V O I
R E O I S O L N A N R T I W
D C R N O M I N A T I O N P
H W O C L A S S I C S N P E
```

Answer on page 107.

Speaking My Language

AFRIKAANS

ALBANIAN

ARABIC

BENGALI

BOSNIAN

CATALAN

DANISH

DUTCH

ENGLISH

ESPERANTO

GERMAN

GREEK

HAITIAN CREOLE

HAWAIIAN

HUNGARIAN

ICELANDIC

JAPANESE

KOREAN

LATIN

LITHUANIAN

MANDARIN

MONGOLIAN

NORWEGIAN

PASHTO

POLISH

PORTUGUESE

SAMOAN

SCOTTISH GAELIC

SERBIAN

SOMALI

URDU

N A I R A G N U H S I L O P
C A T A L A N L I S N B E L
M A E N H D M A U A I G M E
A A N R O A N E I T H N I H
N G N I O N W L E N N G A L
I U R D U K O A C S S I H D
C I L E A G H S I T I O C S
I O P D N R B U B I T I B N
D T N O U D I U A N A T A A
N N M C R T H N R A T N L A
A A S J H T C E A M O Y B K
L R O N A R U H M R E E A I
E E M A E P A G W E N G N R
C P A O N N A E U G R D I F
I S L M R A G N A E G O A A
N E I A F I L L E Y S A N N
O T H S A P I K I S D E M O
S Q U N A I B R E S E I T O
L A T I N A I N A U H T I L

Answer on page 108.

American Revolution

ADAMS

BILL OF RIGHTS

BOSTON TEA PARTY

BUNKER HILL

COLONY

CONSTITUTION

FEDERALIST

FOUNDING FATHERS

FRANKLIN

HAMILTON

INDEPENDENCE DAY

JEFFERSON

KING GEORGE

LIBERTY

LOYALIST

MADISON

MIDNIGHT RIDE

MILITIA

MINUTEMAN

PATRIOTS

REDCOAT

TORY

WASHINGTON

```
P Y N A T A O C D E R P U L
R T C O L O N Y G E A V N E
F R W R S S E R D T I I D Y
L E N A T R O S R H L O T A
L B D U S E E I T K T R H D
I I E E G H O F N B A R I E
H L S G R T I A F P T I S C
R M N T S A R N A E H A C N
E I I R H F L E G N J O L E
K L E D C G T I O T N O O D
N I M I N N I S S O N Y N
U T G H O I I R T T E N A E
B I N T E D G I F F D M L P
E A S D A N T H T O E O I E
S O P M R U E A T T L D S D
B Y R O T O T H U R E L T N
W O R I D F M N O R I E I I
D I O H A M I L T O N D S B
C N R E S M A D A E T L E Y
```

Answer on page 108.

It's Greek to Me

APHRODITE

APOLLO

ARES

ARTEMIS

ATLAS

CASSANDRA

CASSIOPEIA

CHRONOS

CLYTEMNESTRA

EURYDICE

GAIA

HADES

HEPHAESTUS

HERA

HERMES

ICARUS

IPHIGENIA

ODYSSEUS

ORION

ORPHEUS

PANDORA

PENELOPE

PERSEPHONE

PERSEUS

POSEIDON

PROMETHEUS

SISYPHUS

THESEUS

ZEUS

```
E C I D Y R U E O T A H A E
P Y A S E T I D O R H P A A
O S Y I D O Y N O T O I P L
L O E O E S K D A L N G E O
E I F M S P N T L E H A R O
N R S E R A O O G E R P S I
E N U T P E H I E T H U E N
P S M A R E H O S E T U U O
T E O H G P B E U S U T S D
S D R A I U N S E R A P I I
O N I S G M T A H E R C T E
N A O R E O H J A O D N S S
O W N T A P R A M S N T U O
R H Y I E I H E D S A E E P
H L W H C O T O U E S L Z L
C D H A A H V E N E S B T E
E A R T E M I S H E A E N A
A U V U E R Y T G O C O R D
S I S U H P Y S I S D E A A
```

Answer on page 109.

Fly by Night (and also day)

AIRLINER

BIRD

BLIMP

BOX KITE

DRAGONFLY

DRONE

DUMBO

FAIRY

FIGHTER JET

FIREWORKS

FLYING SAUCER

FRISBEE

GHOST

GLIDER

GOLDEN SNITCH

HARPY

HOT-AIR BALLOON

IRON MAN

MAGIC CARPET

SANTA'S REINDEER

SEAPLANE

SPACE STATION

SUPERMAN

TRAPEZE ARTIST

WITCH'S BROOM

```
T  E  J  R  E  T  H  G  I  F  A  I  R  Y
M  A  G  I  C  C  A  R  P  E  T  W  T  H
S  K  R  O  W  E  R  I  F  E  I  F  H  A
E  S  T  E  L  S  P  T  B  T  I  O  R  S
T  F  D  I  D  D  Y  S  C  T  T  H  A  E
I  S  L  R  E  P  E  H  E  A  R  N  E  A
K  G  I  Y  R  I  S  N  I  N  T  E  F  P
X  B  A  T  I  B  L  R  S  A  C  O  N  L
O  B  N  A  R  N  B  N  S  N  D  O  G  A
B  L  T  O  H  A  G  R  E  S  I  L  L  N
O  I  O  W  L  E  E  S  S  T  I  T  T  E
I  M  S  L  A  I  T  Z  A  D  I  S  C  G
E  P  O  B  N  E  T  T  F  U  W  U  E  II
E  O  E  D  N  A  S  R  E  P  C  P  L  O
N  L  E  T  H  E  E  B  B  O  A  E  I  S
O  E  R  D  C  S  T  H  S  A  B  R  R  T
R  T  N  A  M  N  O  R  I  C  A  M  T  N
D  T  P  R  E  N  I  L  R  I  A  A  U  F
L  S  D  R  A  G  O  N  F  L  Y  N  Y  D
```

Answer on page 109.

At the Library

ATLAS

BIOGRAPHY

BOOKS

CALL NUMBER

CATALOG

CIRCULATION

DESK

DUE DATE

ENCYCLOPEDIAS

FANTASY

INTERNET

JUVENILE

LATE FEE

LECTURES

LIBRARIAN

MUSIC

MYSTERIES

NEWSPAPERS

OVERDUE

PHOTOCOPIER

READING

RESEARCH

RESOURCES

ROMANCE

SHELVING CART

STORY TIME

THESAURUS

VIDEOS

YOUNG ADULT

```
E I S R E P A P S W E N H N
E T A D E U D A V U E F A T
F M O S U S N D D T H I E E
E Y G M K O E R S J R T N R
T S N C V O E A U A A C T R
A T I I L V O V R U Y S H E
L E D R O B E B A C O B E T
T R A C G N I V L E H S S N
L I E U I L L O D E T E A I
U E R L H I P I G N C G U I
D S E A L E V N M R Y W R E
A A L T D E L E U E A T U M
G R E I P O C O T O H P S I
N I A O S N S T M Y L I H T
U S B N A E A M U S I C R Y
O A R M R Y C T A R R D L R
Y G O L A T A C L D E S K O
A R E B M U N L L A C S U T
R A B U S F A N T A S Y H S
```

Answer on page 110.

T for Two

TACO TUESDAY

TAG TEAM

TAKE TEN

TALL TALE

TASTE TEST

TATER TOTS

TEA TROLLEY

TEETER-TOTTER

TELL TIME

TEMPER TANTRUM

TENURE TRACK

TESSA THOMPSON

TEXT TONE

TICKER TAPE

TINA TURNER

TOM-TOM

TONGUE TWISTER

TRACTOR-TRAILER

TRAIN TICKET

TREASURE TROVE

TREE TOAD

TURKEY TROT

TURN TAIL

TV TRAY

```
S  T  A  C  O  T  U  E  S  D  A  Y  N  O
W  T  W  H  T  A  M  T  S  E  T  H  E  T  E
T  F  O  O  V  I  T  A  L  L  T  A  L  E
R  R  T  T  T  W  M  O  L  P  K  H  N  V
R  E  A  L  R  S  U  O  E  E  M  O  R  O
E  A  L  N  A  E  R  I  T  N  T  G  E  R
I  E  L  I  Y  T  T  E  N  T  U  T  N  T
T  M  I  T  A  T  N  A  X  E  E  R  R  E
U  A  A  E  C  R  A  E  T  N  O  M  U  R
R  E  T  S  I  W  T  E  U  G  N  O  T  U
K  T  N  N  F  U  R  R  S  I  T  T  A  S
E  G  R  T  R  E  E  T  O  A  D  M  N  A
Y  A  U  O  N  T  P  O  S  T  R  O  I  E
T  T  T  I  R  N  M  T  C  O  C  T  T  R
R  E  P  A  T  R  E  K  C  I  T  A  M  T
O  P  C  L  E  T  T  T  E  D  I  S  R  O
T  K  R  T  E  K  C  I  T  N  I  A  R  T
D  N  O  S  P  M  O  H  T  A  S  S  E  T
R  E  T  T  O  T  R  E  T  E  E  T  E  R
```

Answer on page 110.

Antique Store

ARMOIRE

BASEBALL CARDS

BOTTLES

CAMERA

CANDLESTICKS

CERAMICS

CHAIRS

CHESS SET

CLOCK

COINS

COSTUME JEWELRY

DRESSER

GLASSES

LIGHTER

MIRROR

MUSIC BOX

PICTURE FRAME

PLATES

PORCELAIN

PUNCH BOWL

RADIO

SALT SHAKER

SCULPTURE

SILVERWARE

TEACUPS

TYPEWRITER

WRISTWATCH

```
S  N  L  W  O  B  H  C  N  U  P  O  T  E
K  E  M  A  R  F  E  R  U  T  C  I  P  X
C  V  E  R  Y  I  S  R  I  A  H  C  T  O
I  P  L  A  T  E  S  E  H  I  N  G  S  B
T  Y  P  E  W  R  I  T  E  R  I  D  N  C
S  E  A  C  N  A  N  H  W  T  R  I  Q  I
E  U  R  O  K  S  E  G  L  A  S  S  E  S
L  S  A  I  T  C  O  I  C  R  T  E  I  U
D  S  D  N  O  I  O  L  A  N  S  C  A  M
N  N  I  S  I  M  L  L  T  I  E  Q  H  S
A  C  O  U  E  A  R  B  C  D  L  U  A  P
C  T  H  O  B  R  L  A  R  L  T  L  D  U
Y  R  L  E  W  E  J  E  M  U  T  S  O  C
S  T  S  U  S  C  S  I  C  S  O  F  F  A
S  A  T  O  A  S  R  R  H  R  B  E  D  E
B  O  E  M  E  R  S  A  S  N  O  T  H  T
A  V  E  R  O  E  K  E  T  H  E  P  S  A
M  R  E  R  R  E  R  U  T  P  L  U  C  S
A  I  N  E  R  A  W  R  E  V  L  I  S  G
```

Answer on page 111.

On the Road

BACK-SEAT DRIVER

BRAKES

BRIDGE

DAY TRIP

DETOUR

EXIT

FREEWAY

GARAGE

GETAWAY

HAIRPIN TURNS

HYBRID

INTERSTATE

LICENSE

LUGGAGE

PARKWAY

RAMP

REST AREA

ROUTE SIXTY-SIX

SEAT BELT

SERVICE STATION

SIGHTSEEING

SIGN

SPEED LIMIT

TRAFFIC

TRAVEL

TUNNEL

VACATION

VISIT

```
R R Y I N E G D I R B I C F
Y E O A O O U D E O N N I D
T H V U W S I G N T A V F A
E E Y I T E R T E O O U F Y
S G R D R E E R A R I U A T
N V A E R D S R S C L W R R
R O I R C T T I F E A N T I
U S I E A Y A A X T E V T P
T L A T N G R D E T I S I V
N U E Y A O E G U S Y W A L
I G N N T T A T P O K S I G
P G S O N F S E X I T C I O
R A R E A U E E S P E I A X
I G R N A D T T C N H E R B
A E E K L T S A S I L W R A
H Y S I W A B E L E V A R T
R A M P M A E E R R K R Y G
D I R B Y H Y O L E R O E U
T N D G N I E E S T H G I S
```

Answer on page 111.

World Traveler

ATHENS

BARCELONA

BIRMINGHAM

BUENOS AIRES

COPENHAGEN

DAR ES SALAAM

HELSINKI

ISTANBUL

JAKARTA

JERUSALEM

LILLEHAMMER

MANILA

MECCA

MELBOURNE

MONTEVIDEO

MONTREAL

PHILADELPHIA

SAN FRANCISCO

SANTO DOMINGO

SÃO PAULO

SHANGHAI

STOCKHOLM

VANCOUVER

WARSAW

ZURICH

```
W A H A L A E R T N O M T T
W O C S I C N A R F N A S E
S T O C K H O L M O I A F N
A A S O E U C R L H E L R R
O T N I T M T I P E B A E U
P R E T K R W L R U O S V O
A A H R O N E L E U R S U B
U K T D C D I N I E Z E O L
L A A L A T O S M I E R C E
O J S L U S C M L A N A N M
N B I E A B A S I E C D A E
R H A I M H N A G N H H V L
P B R L E E H A D T G O G A
E E T L H G H E T N R O M S
S T L O N N M A I S K E A U
T I H A E E W M O R I D N R
L M H P W A R S A W E M I E
O S O E D I V E T N O M L J
R C I A B A R C E L O N A L
```

Answer on page 112.

A Silly Puzzle

ABSURD

ASININE

BALDERDASH

BALMY

BIZARRE

CLOWNISH

COMICAL

CRACKPOT

CUCKOO

DEMENTED

ECCENTRIC

FARCICAL

FLAKY

FOOLISH

FUNNY

HUMOROUS

LOONY

LUDICROUS

MADCAP

NONSENSICAL

NUTTY

OFF THE WALL

OUTLANDISH

PREPOSTEROUS

QUIRKY

RIDICULOUS

SCREWBALL

WEIRD

ZANY

```
S  B  H  S  I  D  N  A  L  T  U  O  I  A
P  R  I  D  I  C  U  L  O  U  S  L  S  L
A  Y  S  Z  T  R  A  I  N  G  W  I  A  S
C  I  N  V  A  B  C  L  O  W  N  I  S  H
D  R  I  E  W  R  E  N  T  I  E  D  B  Y
A  P  A  E  C  C  R  I  N  D  E  H  N  T
M  B  R  B  A  L  D  E  R  D  A  S  H  Q
Y  C  P  E  E  O  D  C  P  L  L  I  D  U
S  E  B  L  P  T  R  C  R  Y  O  L  E  I
U  S  A  L  I  O  U  E  N  G  Y  O  T  R
O  U  L  A  C  I  S  N  E  S  N  O  N  K
R  O  M  W  T  C  B  T  O  P  A  F  E  Y
O  R  Y  E  R  O  A  R  F  O  Z  D  M  N
M  C  U  H  Y  M  C  I  E  R  A  O  E  N
U  I  S  T  P  I  R  C  Y  A  O  Y  D  U
H  D  T  F  O  C  N  C  A  K  S  U  T  F
F  U  O  F  L  A  C  I  R  A  F  S  R
N  L  S  O  P  L  R  U  A  I  N  L  E  D
L  I  T  O  P  K  C  A  R  C  M  B  F  S
```

Answer on page 112.

Olympic Sports

ARCHERY

BADMINTON

BMX RACING

BOBSLED

BOXING

CURLING

EQUESTRIAN

FENCING

FIGURE SKATING

GOLF

HANDBALL

HOCKEY

KARATE

LUGE

NORDIC COMBINED

ROWING

RUGBY

SAILING

SKELETON

SWIMMING

TAEKWONDO

TENNIS

TRAMPOLINE

TRIATHLON

VOLLEYBALL

WATER POLO

WEIGHTLIFTING

```
N O L H T A I R T S E P O R
N T D S H O C K E Y S G F E
A T T N V O D E A B U I U F
I R T B O X I N G R G A N L
R T C T L W H E T U A W O O
T B E H L N K D R G T T T G
S M G Y E T W E E B N T E N
E X N Y Y R S N A Y F E L I
U R I O B K Y I U T N R E T
Q A M P A A R B N I I S K F
E C M T L O O M L N L F S I
Y I I M L B P O I C E S A L
I N W N S C P C L N U T I T
G G S L D M E C C B R E L H
N A E K A G N I L R U C I G
I D D R H A N D B A L L N I
W A T N C G I R N G A N G E
O D S U R O L O P R E T A W
R F I N N O T N I M D A B G
```

Answer on page 113.

Wide World of Color

AMBER

AQUAMARINE

AUBURN

BURNT UMBER

CELADON

CERISE

CERULEAN

CHARTREUSE

CHESTNUT

CINNABAR

COBALT

CRIMSON

GOLDENROD

INDIGO

LAPIS LAZULI

LAVENDER

MAROON

MAUVE

MUSTARD

OCHRE

ORCHID

PERIWINKLE

PERSIMMON

PUCE

ROBIN'S-EGG BLUE

SAPPHIRE

TANGERINE

TURQUOISE

VERMILION

```
D S N O B V E R M I L I O N
W I M Y T U N T S E H C O E
G R H U E T R S H O U M S E
F I N C S C N N H E M I C E
R S R A R T N O T I L D E S
E O E O A O A O S U C O R I
S M B G B M O R Z M M N I O
U M M I A Y E A D N I B S U
E A A D N P L M S P A R E Q
R S L N N S S O E L A Y C R
T B A I I C E R U L E A N U
R L U P C E I G M E G A G T
A E A S P W A A G S U D O N
H L D T I H U C O B A L T O
C H E N B V I L U U L E P D
J A K Y E N I R A M A U Q A
A L N D B V N L E U C E E L
E R H C O T A N G E R I N E
B D O R N E D L O G I R D C
```

Answer on page 113.

What's Your Hobby?

ANIME

ANTIQUING

ASTROLOGY

BIRDWATCHING

BOWLING

CHESS

DIORAMA

FILM

FOSSILS

GENEALOGY

GEOCACHING

GOLF

JUDO

KARAOKE

METAL DETECTION

MODEL TRAINS

ORIGAMI

PHOTOGRAPHY

PIANO

POLO

QUILTING

SEWING

SHORTWAVE RADIO

SLOT CARS

TAROT

TENNIS

TOPIARY

TRIVIA

WORD SEARCHES

YOGA

ZUMBA

```
A  I  G  G  O  L  F  F  Y  Y  J  O  U  S
R  B  H  N  O  O  T  A  R  O  T  U  H  B
G  Y  M  I  I  B  N  A  Y  R  I  O  D  F
N  G  G  U  S  H  I  A  I  B  R  Y  I  O
I  O  N  Q  Z  P  C  V  I  T  H  L  O  S
W  L  I  I  O  W  I  T  W  P  M  L  E  S
E  A  T  T  I  A  N  A  A  G  T  H  M  I
S  E  L  N  C  H  V  R  A  W  C  O  T  L
M  N  I  A  E  E  G  A  N  R  D  S  G  S
Y  E  U  Y  R  O  T  S  A  E  O  R  N  U
G  G  Q  A  T  E  L  E  L  N  K  J  I  O
O  Y  D  O  M  O  S  T  D  A  O  A  L  B
L  I  H  O  T  D  R  K  R  I  I  L  W  N
O  P  G  C  R  A  S  A  S  S  A  P  O  A
R  R  A  O  I  I  O  S  E  I  S  T  B  P
T  R  W  N  A  K  G  I  E  N  N  Y  E  O
S  U  S  G  E  O  C  A  C  H  I  N  G  M
A  R  O  S  P  A  N  I  M  E  C  A  E  R
E  Y  T  I  A  M  A  R  O  I  D  M  E  T
```

Answer on page 114.

Fun and Games

APPLES TO APPLES

CANDY LAND

CASINO

CHECKERS

CHESS

CHUTES AND LADDERS

CLUE

CONNECT FOUR

CRIBBAGE

DOMINOES

GO FISH

HEARTS

JENGA

MASTERMIND

MOUSE TRAP

OLD MAID

PINOCHLE

RISK

SCRABBLE

SORRY!

SPADES

STRATEGO

TABOO

TICKET TO RIDE

TRIVIAL PURSUIT

TWISTER

WHIST

YAHTZEE

```
B E D I R O T T E K C I T O
G O F I S H E F W O P R N E
T I U S R U P L A I V I R T
T A G N E J S H N I S N K S
I D N G D E O O F A T T E H
E E N N D A C M C E S L E C
L R A A A H E B B L P O W R
B E P I L T Y G S P I L H N
B S V E D Y E R A N T D I O
A R T M N R D O R B I M S S
R E D T A P T N O O B A T R
C H E S S S A H A E S I N E
S T R A E H T R A C M D R K
E S C L T O G E T A R T S C
R I P S U S C R R E O S S E
W P Y A H T Z E E M S O R H
A D S A C L U E N D I U L C
K S I R U O F T C E N N O C
E X I C O S E O N I M O D M
```

Answer on page 114.

Remember When

ANCESTRY

AULD LANG SYNE

BYGONE

CULTURE

CUSTOM

GOLDEN AGE

HALCYON

HERITAGE

HOME MOVIES

HOMETOWN

IDYLLIC

LEGACY

MEMORIES

MISS

MYTH

NOSTALGIA

PAST

PHOTO ALBUM

RELIC

REMINISCING

SCRAPBOOK

SENTIMENTAL

THE GOOD OLD DAYS

TIME IMMEMORIAL

TRADITION

YESTERYEAR

```
M E E N M E O Y C A G E L R
C Y N O I S G I T N H P E S
D I M Y T H L A I I H A R S
N Y L C S E W C N O P E Y I
O A A L R G S L T E L A C M
I A I A Y I N O R R D Y S A
T H R H N D A A B D O L U T
I O O I T L I W L S I T O H
D M M U B S O O E D S S S G
A E E U H C D I A E L R C E
R T M N W O R I N L D U R N
T O M E O O M T C I N U A O
T W I G M S I E H U T E D G
I N E E M M T P M L S O B Y
R H M T E A N A U O C T O B
T E I N O F B C L E V I O N
G E T H E R I T A G E I K M
R A E Y R E T S E Y I A E R
L N E S Y R T S E C N A T S
```

Answer on page 115.

Feeling Good

AMIABLE

BLITHE

BUCOLIC

BUOYANT

CALM

CAREFREE

CHEERY

CONFIDENT

CONTENT

ELATED

EQUABLE

EUPHORIC

EVEN-KEELED

GLAD

HAPPY-GO-LUCKY

HARMONIOUS

JAUNTY

JOVIAL

LAID-BACK

ON CLOUD NINE

OVERJOYED

PACIFIC

RELAXED

RESTFUL

ROSY

SANGUINE

SEDATE

SERENE

SUNNY

UNDISTURBED

```
I  F  K  C  A  B  D  I  A  L  Y  C  O  R
E  U  T  H  I  I  E  N  K  C  I  L  E  O
T  O  U  C  A  L  M  D  N  F  I  S  C  S
A  N  H  E  B  I  O  S  I  T  T  D  O  Y
D  E  X  A  L  E  R  C  O  F  S  E  N  O
E  C  U  R  P  O  A  W  U  U  D  T  F  T
S  Q  E  D  W  P  E  L  O  B  H  A  I  N
E  J  A  U  N  T  Y  I  A  E  A  L  D  A
N  R  G  O  S  A  N  G  U  I  N  E  E  Y
I  O  E  C  D  O  T  H  O  I  V  V  N  O
N  N  L  I  M  G  S  A  B  L  E  O  T  U
D  E  B  R  U  T  S  I  D  N  U  O  J  B
U  U  A  O  T  C  L  O  K  A  U  C  L  D
O  H  I  H  S  S  C  E  O  N  L  I  K  E
L  S  M  P  T  H  E  W  O  F  T  G  I  Y
C  U  A  U  E  L  V  R  E  H  S  E  V  E
N  N  N  E  E  C  A  R  E  F  R  E  E  A
O  N  R  D  N  D  E  C  O  N  T  E  N  T
I  Y  G  H  D  E  Y  O  J  R  E  V  O  T
```

Answer on page 115.

On the Farm

AGRICULTURE

BARN

CHICKEN

COMBINE

CORN

CREAM

CROP ROTATION

CULTIVATOR

DUCKLINGS

FERTILIZER

FLOCK

FRUIT

GRAIN

GREENHOUSE

HOMESTEAD

HONEYBEE

HYDROPONIC

IRRIGATION

LONGHORN

ORGANIC

PASTURE

PICK YOUR OWN

RANCH

SCARECROW

SEEDS

SHEPHERD

STALLION

VEGETABLE

```
D S S N R O H G N O L V C A
R R D E H O M E S T E A D C
E R O E W S T O R G A N I C
H F A G E R E A E E I X R S
P T E R R S E T V A M N A G
E A E R U E A L R I O Y N N
H G S O T B E G O I T E C I
S D A T L I T N T T K L H L
H N E E U I L A H C R Y U K
E J W N C R T I I O D O B C
N T R O I O E H Z R U H E U
I A F Y R A C E O E R S E D
B K L P G U N P B O R W E M
M N O N A T O O B Y E O A U
O R C R T N S Y T A E E N F
C D K O I I N G K I R N R N
W O R C E R A C S C T U O H
E N O I T A G I R R I I R H
F I E N O I L L A T S P L D
```

Answer on page 116.

Bling

ALLOY

AQUAMARINE

BIRTHSTONE

BROOCH

CHAIN

CHARM

CROWN

CRYSTAL

CUFFLINKS

DROP EARRINGS

ENGAGEMENT RING

ENGRAVING

FACET

GARNET

GOLD

HAIRPIN

HOOP

LAPIS LAZULI

LOCKET

NECKLACE

ONYX

OPAL

PENDANT

PLATINUM

RUBY

SILVER

STAR SAPPHIRE

TURQUOISE

```
C T H P E N D A N T E C A F
H U O C Y N E C G U L L M I
C O F N O A O N N T D U I E
H A M F L O I T U O N N N D
A C I S L V R R S I T G H E
R R D E A I Q B T H A L R A
M O R R P U N A G G I I E S
T W G I O N L K E T H R H E
I N W I N P O M S P R L I D
E L S U Y N E L P I E S E B
S E U Y X N I A H C L N O T
U M E Z T A S N R B I V A E
D S E R A R B I H R A L E N
L L I D A L I A A M I O N R
O N D T O S S M I T B N E A
G C S C A U A I R S S E G G
T H K O R U B Y P S E Y A S
R E E M Q U C H I A B I R G
T E C A L K C E N G L E R C
```

Answer on page 116.

Ten-Spots

ADOLESCENT

ASTROLOGER

ATMOSPHERE

BEWILDERED

CHINCHILLA

COMMERCIAL

CURMUDGEON

ECHINODERM

ECONOMICAL

EUCALYPTUS

FAHRENHEIT

HOODWINKED

LARYNGITIS

MULTIMEDIA

NINCOMPOOP

OVERRIDING

PALINDROME

PARANORMAL

PIGEONHOLE

RHINOCEROS

SWITCHEROO

THERMOSTAT

WAVELENGTH

WEIGHTIEST

```
N A D I P O O P M O C N I N
A T A T S O M R E H T C O M
L A R Y N G I T I S A N F D
E T C I O E F N R O M A A E
L N S O R E C O N I H R I K
A A W E A H S S T R H E N N
M E S W I T C H E R O O F I
R U I L H T G N E L E V A W
O C L R R S H T G G O Y M D
N A A T N E A G D S M D P O
A L I T I T G U I R O A A O
R Y C T S M M O E E L C O H
A P R D E R E D L I W E B R
P T E E U A O D N O P E R F
E U M C G N I D I R R E V O
C S M T I T R E N A A T T T
E L O H N O E G I P H E S O
L A C I M O N O C E L Y M A
P E R E H P S O M T A I C S
```

Answer on page 117.

Red, Red, and More Red

APPLE

BARN

CHILI PEPPER

CRANBERRIES

DRAGON FRUIT

FIRE HYDRANT

GARNET

GERANIUM

HEART

KIDNEY BEANS

LADYBUG

LIPSTICK

LOBSTER

MACAW

MARS

POMEGRANATE

POPPY

RADISH

RARE STEAK

RUBY SLIPPERS

SALSA

SANTA'S SUIT

SPAGHETTI SAUCE

STOP SIGN

TRAFFIC LIGHT

WATERMELON

WINE

```
T I W A S T S T O P S I G N
N N S R T G E R A N I U M C
K T A O B L E N A D I F H S
C M L R F A E E R R E I P N
I T S I D D B F N A L A T E
T V A E R Y Y O N I G W I E
S R I S E B H R P H W A U S
P W A N E U A E E R I T R E
I N D F G G P T R B L E F I
L I A C F P T S K I P R N R
K I W A E I P B N P F M O R
A A T R S T C O I O H E G E
P W E A B E W I P S E L A B
P A U T A R S I I P N O R N
L C G R S Y E D D G Y N D A
E A B M B E A A R I H A S R
H M A U A R R H E A R T R C
A P R S A N T A S S U I T O
V A N E T A N A R G E M O P
```

Answer on page 117.

Wild West

BANDIT

BRONCO

CACTUS

CATTLE DRIVE

COWBOY HAT

CRITTER

FRONTIER

HOMESTEAD

LASSO

MULE

OUTLAW

PIONEER

PLAINS

PONY EXPRESS

PROSPECTOR

RANCHER

RANGE BOSS

RAWHIDE

RODEO

ROUNDUP

SALOON

SHERIFF

STAGECOACH

STAKE A CLAIM

TUMBLEWEED

WAGON TRAIN

```
R E H C N A R D B D I L S L
L C A C T U S A E Y P T A H
P S N I A L P E E R K S L C
R O D E O O W T O I S D O W
A S N A N E C S O O U W O T
L A W Y L F P E O R B J N C
R E U B E E S M G O T S A I
E L M X C X S O Y A Y T E A
I U R T S H P H B E T F O M
T M O N E R A R W L E S I P
N R B R I T R E E A I A N U
O G I K I A L D L S L E D D
R F C A W T R T T C S T O N
F H R H E I A T A G E C U U
O F I T V D W E N E N N T O
Y D T E O N K P I O N E E R
E N T E B A Y S R H G E R I
F F E P T B A B T G A A R R
E T R S S O B E G N A R W T
```

Answer on page 118.

Very Online

BOOKMARK

BROADBAND

BROWSER

CHATROOM

CODE

COOKIE

CYBERSPACE

DATA

DOMAIN NAME

DOWNLOAD

EMAILS

FORUM

HACKER

HOMEPAGE

HOTSPOT

HTML

IN REAL LIFE

INSTAGRAM

LIVE STREAMER

NETIQUETTE

PODCASTING

REDDIT

SEARCH ENGINE

TECH SUPPORT

THUMBNAIL

TRENDING

WEBCAM

WIFI

WIRELESS

```
T H I E S D O W N L O A D B
F O D T R E N D I N G O O L
K O O N R F W A S L I A M E
C B R O A O N R D E S T A L
S E R U A B P R C C H H I E
S E E O M S D P M A M V N T
E A A U W Y N A U P E W N T
L F H R O S R T O S B E A E
E T I E C G E D T R H B M U
R T E L A H C R C E B C E Q
I H N T L A E O L B O A E I
W G S I S A C N A Y L M I T
L N Y T M A E D G C V A K E
I N I E C E D R W I F I O N
B N R U T I E N N A N W O A
G K R A M K O O B I Y E C A
I T I S C H A T R O O M T W
I E G A P E M O H R E A L E
S S H O T S P O T I D D E R
```

Answer on page 118.

Romantic Comedies

AMÉLIE

ARTHUR

BORN YESTERDAY

CLUELESS

DESK SET

GROUNDHOG DAY

HITCH

JUNO

LEAP YEAR

LOVE, SIMON

MARRY ME

MEET CUTE

MOONSTRUCK

ONLY YOU

PALM SPRINGS

PILLOW TALK

PRETTY WOMAN

ROMAN HOLIDAY

ROXANNE

SABRINA

SOME LIKE IT HOT

SPLASH

THE APARTMENT

THE GOODBYE GIRL

WALL-E

YOU'VE GOT MAIL

```
T  S  G  N  I  R  P  S  M  L  A  P  T  H
N  E  P  R  K  L  A  T  W  O  L  L  I  P
E  E  L  L  S  C  B  E  M  Y  R  R  A  M
M  O  L  I  A  T  U  H  Y  A  R  Y  U  E
T  S  R  R  A  S  O  R  M  P  A  C  O  T
R  A  I  U  O  M  H  M  T  D  A  A  Y  U
A  B  G  H  N  D  T  T  G  S  A  E  Y  C
P  R  E  T  T  Y  W  O  M  A  N  H  L  T
A  I  Y  R  O  R  H  H  G  R  O  O  N  E
E  N  B  A  R  D  F  T  I  E  L  M  O  E
H  A  D  N  N  O  M  I  S  E  V  O  L  M
T  A  O  U  M  E  D  E  M  O  T  U  H  E
R  S  O  D  T  E  S  K  S  F  D  A  O  Y
S  R  G  N  O  D  O  I  L  N  T  G  E  Y
G  T  E  T  U  H  C  L  U  E  L  E  S  S
E  W  H  R  O  J  A  E  N  N  A  X  O  R
H  C  T  I  H  W  A  M  E  L  I  E  N  G
O  N  Y  A  D  I  L  O  H  N  A  M  O  R
E  B  O  R  N  Y  E  S  T  E  R  D  A  Y
```

Answer on page 119.

Spa Day

BLOW-DRY

BLUSH

BRAID

BRONZER

BRUSH

CLEANSER

CONCEALER

COVER-UP

CREAM

EMERY BOARD

EXFOLIATE

EYESHADOW

FACIAL

FOUNDATION

GLOSS

HAIRLINE

LIPSTICK

LOTION

MAKEOVER

MOISTURIZER

POWDER

RINSE

ROUGE

SALON

SAUNA

SHAMPOO

STRAIGHTEN

STYLIST

TANNING

TWEEZERS

WEAVE

```
A F S H A I R L I N E D B P
E V A E W A R W I X T R H S
O B M C E B O E F N U A N E
K O L N I R S O Z S T O A S
F C F O W A L H H N I B O R
I S I R W I L E A T O Y L E
N O I T A D N U O F L R Y Z
E R G T S R R L E A H E B E
T T E A T P G Y P S T M M E
H A S Z S N I S U O R E O W
G R A S I A G L E E W O O T
I E U N L R B S V C P D O U
A L N L Y D U O P M A R E O
R A A M T O E T A H T E T R
T E H E S K M H S R I N S E
S C L E A N S E R I A S S T
H N E M W I Y Z A N O L A S
R O P U R E V O C L D M O F
A C R E A M A E G U O R H S
```

Answer on page 119.

It's Showtime!

ANNIE

BARNUM

CABARET

CAROUSEL

CHESS

CHICAGO

COMPANY

CRAZY FOR YOU

DREAMGIRLS

EVITA

FALSETTOS

GODSPELL

GRAND HOTEL

GREASE

GUYS AND DOLLS

HAMILTON

HELLO, DOLLY!

MAMMA MIA!

MISS SAIGON

NEWSIES

OKLAHOMA!

OLIVER!

ONCE ON THIS ISLAND

RENT

SEUSSICAL

SHE LOVES ME

SHOW BOAT

SWEET CHARITY

```
H A G R E A S E I S W E N M
I L T O O A M O H A L K O N
S L L O D D N A S Y U G E A
Y R N E N S M A M M A M I A
L D T H A I P E M C O S C Y
L A S T L T O E I N Y H O T
O A C T S E W H L S A O M I
D R O I I D C N O L C W P R
O N M N S S E H C R I B A A
L G N M I S S S A I G O N H
L A R T H N U Z A G T A Y C
E R N A T I Y E O M N T A T
H E S B N F U T S A T B M L
R V H E O D P R O E A D U E
U I C R E E H R S R H A N W
S L Y T C H E O E D M O R S
S O T W N S O T T E S L A F
U C A R O U S E L E I N B S
A T I V E M S E V O L E H S
```

Answer on page 120.

Fine Arts

ABSTRACT

AVANT-GARDE

BACKGROUND

BRUSH

CANVAS

COMPOSITION

CONTEMPORARY

CURATOR

DADA

DESIGN

DRAWING

ETCHING

EXHIBITION

FORM

FRAME

IMAGE

IMPRESSIONIST

INSTALLATION

LANDSCAPE

MINIMALISM

PAINTER

PASTEL

PIGMENT

PORTRAIT

POSE

SCENE

STILL LIFE

SURREAL

WATERCOLOR

```
E E A P L Q U G N I H C T E
D G N I W A R D A D A O T F
R A E G F R E T O M R O F I
A M E M M E C R S D W A N L
G I P E N A R I R W D S G L
T H A N R O L S A U T O I L
N P C T P A I T C A S E S I
A R S O M I E T L E I F E T
V B D I N R Y L I B N N D S
A O N U C T A C A B O E O U
L I A O D T E C S I I A Y P
M I L T I I K M T N S H O W
O O R O D G S I P I S S X T
R S N H R E S R E O E E W E
O A U O L O D T B B R U S H
E V U N P O S R E A P A S O
N N T M O A P F R A M E R A
D A O I P O R T R A I T N Y
T C U R A T O R E T N I A P
```

Answer on page 120.

Back to School

BACKPACK

BUSES

CAFETERIA

CHORUS

CLASSROOMS

CLUBS

ERASER

FIELD TRIP

GRADE

GRAMMAR

GYMNASIUM

HALL MONITOR

HIGHLIGHTER

LEARN

LIBRARY

LUNCH

PENCIL

PLAYGROUND

RECESS

RULER

SCIENCE FAIR

SHOW AND TELL

SPELLING

SUBSTITUTE

TEACHER

TEST

TIMES TABLE

```
I  R  E  H  C  A  E  T  F  T  H  H  E  C
H  E  I  G  R  A  M  M  A  R  A  L  D  S
B  R  L  I  S  N  F  O  T  L  L  E  S  S
A  A  R  B  N  R  A  E  L  N  I  E  U  N
G  S  C  T  A  H  E  M  T  W  C  R  A  M
S  E  Y  K  Y  T  O  O  U  E  O  A  L  U
M  R  R  E  P  N  S  T  R  H  R  L  E  I
O  A  C  R  I  A  F  E  C  N  E  I  C  S
O  H  B  T  E  I  C  N  M  T  G  T  A  A
R  S  O  U  H  T  E  K  D  I  N  Y  O  N
S  R  U  U  S  M  H  N  U  S  T  T  F  M
S  T  E  B  A  E  A  G  C  R  H  I  I  Y
A  N  U  T  S  W  S  H  I  U  E  E  W  G
L  L  A  E  O  T  G  N  I  L  L  E  P  S
C  Y  T  H  D  H  I  E  D  E  H  C  H  H
I  T  S  E  T  A  L  T  D  R  L  G  C  E
A  P  L  A  Y  G  R  O  U  N  D  N  I  R
Y  R  A  R  B  I  L  G  N  T  U  S  R  H
I  T  A  D  P  E  N  C  I  L  E  U  N  N
```

Answer on page 121.

Music, Music, Music

A CAPPELLA

ALTERNATIVE

BARBERSHOP

BEBOP

BIG BAND

CAJUN

CALYPSO

CELTIC

CLASSICAL

COUNTRY

DANCE

DELTA BLUES

DISCO

DOO-WOP

DUBSTEP

EASY LISTENING

ELECTRO SWING

GOSPEL

GRUNGE

HEAVY METAL

HOUSE

INSPIRATIONAL

INSTRUMENTAL

JAZZ

LATIN

LULLABY

NEW WAVE

OPERA

ROCK

SOUL

```
P O H S R E B R A B A G C R
E B A O S E U L B A T L E D
T M E M U G Y F L O A R O B
S E S B R S T L D S R O C K
B I I U O G E S S C W E O S
U O N N O P G I W O L A D S
D G G S P I C V P E E I A G
E N P A P A O A C N S C N E
L E C L L I Y T J C O I C V
L A N A C E R I O U N T E I
T W T A L O S A W E N L O T
D Y N E S Y B Y T G L E O A
N R B W M I P S A I C C N N
A G I A A Y I S L U O S I R
B N Y N L L V O O R U N T E
G F O R Y L I A P W N I A T
I I N S T R U M E N T A L L
B J A Z Z L L L R H R S U A
R E V A W W E N A V Y I V E
```

Answer on page 121.

Quiet, Please!

DISHWASHER

FASHION SHOW

KOSHER

MISHMASH

ON A SHORT LEASH

OSHKOSH

ROSH HASHANAH

SHADOW

SHAGGY

SHANGRI-LA

SHAVING BRUSH

SHEEPISH

SHELLAC

SHELLFISH

SHERIFF

SHISH KEBAB

SHOESHINE

SHOOTING STAR

SHORT SHORTS

SHOSHONE

SHOWMANSHIP

SHUFFLED

THRESHER SHARK

WASH ASHORE

WISHY-WASHY

```
E  S  R  A  T  S  G  N  I  T  O  O  H  S
R  E  N  O  H  S  O  H  S  H  E  S  E  L
O  P  I  H  S  N  A  M  W  O  H  S  L  S
H  S  E  D  A  H  S  H  E  H  L  L  S  O
S  B  A  E  Y  S  H  O  E  S  H  I  N  E
A  H  L  L  T  H  E  A  S  O  E  A  S  A
H  S  I  F  L  L  E  H  S  K  S  S  H  H
S  U  R  F  H  O  R  E  K  H  H  B  E  S
A  R  G  U  S  H  U  O  O  S  A  T  L  T
W  B  N  H  I  S  S  R  H  O  D  N  L  R
S  G  A  S  P  H  T  A  O  U  O  L  A  O
H  N  H  B  E  L  D  N  M  T  W  S  C  H
A  I  S  R  E  H  S  A  W  H  S  I  D  S
G  V  H  A  H  K  E  S  E  L  S  L  H  T
G  A  S  E  S  R  H  S  H  E  L  I  L  R
Y  H  S  A  W  Y  H  S  I  W  S  E  M  O
L  S  S  E  W  H  F  F  I  R  E  H  S  H
T  H  R  E  S  H  E  R  S  H  A  R  K  S
E  R  W  O  H  S  N  O  I  H  S  A  F  E
```

Answer on page 122.

These Make Scents

APPLE

BALSAM

CARDAMOM

CINNAMON

CITRUS

COCONUT

CORIANDER

EUCALYPTUS

FRANKINCENSE

GARDENIA

GINGERBREAD

HIBISCUS

HONEYSUCKLE

JASMINE

JUNIPER

LEMON

LILAC

LILY

MAGNOLIA

ORANGE

PASSIONFRUIT

PATCHOULI

PEPPERMINT

PINE

PUMPKIN SPICE

ROSE

SAFFRON

SAGE

SANDALWOOD

```
Y O A I L O N G A M U C A H
N M A P I N E G N A R O I K
C S U T P Y L A C U E B E N
A I E P O L Y T P L I O T O
L S T C U L E R K S R C N R
I A R R I I W C C E O I I F
L N T L U P U U D C M E M F
H D D R I S S N O A E G R A
I A A D Y R A N S O S A E S
L L E E P I U L I E N S P T
U W N A R T A M L K S L P A
O O V O E B O N I D P E E R
H O C R O M R N S I F M P R
C D M A A R C E Y C E L U E
T O V D E E S A G N D M O P
A E R R N O M A N N I C O I
P A S S I O N F R U I T A N
C N E O A I N E D R A G G U
E P E E R L S E N I M S A J
```

Answer on page 122.

Take Me to Your Leader

ALDERMAN

BARONESS

BISHOP

CAPTAIN

CHANCELLOR

CHIEF

COACH

COMMISSIONER

CONGRESSMAN

CONSUL

DALAI LAMA

ELDER

EMIR

EMPEROR

FIRST SELECTMAN

GENERAL

GOVERNOR

IMAM

KING

PASTOR

PHARAOH

POPE

PRESIDENT

PRIME MINISTER

QUEEN

RABBI

REPRESENTATIVE

SUPERVISOR

VICEROY

```
I  R  E  N  O  I  S  S  I  M  M  O  C  F
Y  O  U  A  L  D  E  R  M  A  N  A  A  R
E  I  B  B  A  R  E  E  L  O  P  Q  C  O
K  V  R  I  A  G  N  T  G  T  U  T  H  F
Y  M  I  O  O  R  N  S  A  E  P  U  I  R
O  C  A  T  R  C  O  I  E  H  A  R  E  S
R  O  M  M  A  E  N  N  K  E  S  S  F  N
E  A  A  O  I  T  P  I  E  T  M  E  A  R
C  C  L  S  A  R  N  M  S  S  O  M  E  M
I  H  I  A  U  T  I  E  E  C  S  D  W  O
V  O  A  D  Y  P  L  M  S  S  L  O  U  P
C  H  L  N  O  E  E  I  E  E  G  U  R  A
L  O  A  L  C  D  I  R  N  O  R  E  S  S
A  A  D  T  T  E  G  P  V  E  S  P  L  T
R  R  M  A  M  N  L  E  O  I  D  U  E  O
E  A  S  I  O  A  R  L  D  H  S  Y  P  R
N  H  R  C  T  N  A  E  O  N  S  O  K  E
E  P  M  E  O  T  N  O  O  R  P  I  R  Y
G  O  U  R  R  T  C  C  E  E  D  A  B  R
```

Answer on page 123.

Birdwatching

ALBATROSS

CANADA GOOSE

CARDINAL

CORMORANT

CROW

CUCKOO

DUCK

GRACKLE

GREAT EGRET

GULL

HAWK

KINGFISHER

MOUNTAIN WREN

MOURNING DOVE

ORIOLE

OYSTERCATCHER

PARAKEET

PELICAN

PIGEON

QUAIL

RAVEN

ROBIN

SCREECH OWL

SPARROW

STARLING

STORK

SWAN

TERN

THRUSH

WOODPECKER

```
A H U N R E T H R U S H C M
T E R G E T A E R G M U I N
N G A B S I R D E W C E I O
A G V W O R C H S K S L Y E
R S E L O I R O O T A S S T
O H N A G O N O A A T R N I
M M C K A E D R L E W H A E
R L O I D L L P R E A N V P
O W Q U A I L C E A A O N N
C O O S N T A R L C D I I C
H H W G A T E B I G K I B G
K C U D C H A L N S L E O S
R E M H O T E I R A L E R W
O E E T R P N H N K A N O A
T R T O I R W I C W E R N N
S C S G U T D A Y K R T H L
O S E O U R R S W A A E L N
D O M N A G I A P C K U N F
N L S C R E H S I F G N I K
```

Answer on page 123.

It's Wine O'Clock

APPELLATION

BALANCE

BORDEAUX

BOUQUET

CABERNET

CELLAR

CHAMPAGNE

CHARDONNAY

CHIANTI

CLARET

CORKSCREW

DECANTER

GRENACHE

MADEIRA

MARSALA

MERLOT

MUSCAT

RIESLING

SANGIOVESE

SAUTERNES

SAUVIGNON BLANC

SOMMELIER

SYRAH

VINEYARD

VINTAGE

WINE GLASS

ZINFANDEL

```
B E S C O M T E U Q U O B V
I N G S O M M E L I E R I C
M A R S A L A A R M A N N Z
S C T R A L L E C A T A E I
R H S O D M G M E A L L I N
E I A Y R R I E G B S C S F
S A O R A G R E N A C H E A
E N D I Y N F O F I I C M N
N T U L E S N T B T W U T D
R I S A N G I O V E S E H E
E G A T I O R N D C N L N L
T Y N V V D B E A R F G I V
U E U I E A C T E P A F R M
A A C A L A E B N P T H A E
S O U A N S A F M A P D C R
P X N T L C E A I C E A N L
T C E S P A H I S I S T H O
E R W E R C S K R O C E T T
E S T N O I T A L L E P P A
```

Answer on page 124.

Anagram Pairs

ADVERB	BRAVED
ALLERGY	GALLERY
BLISTER	BRISTLE
CATERER	TERRACE
CAUTIONED	EDUCATION
CLAIMED	MEDICAL
CRUMPETS	SPECTRUM
DRAINAGE	GARDENIA
EARTHLING	LATHERING
EMIRATES	STEAMIER
HARMONICAS	MARASCHINO
HUSTLING	SUNLIGHT
INTEGRAL	TRIANGLE
MAGENTA	NAMETAG
MARACAS	MASCARA
PERCUSSION	SUPERSONIC

```
A I N E D R A G A T E M A N
W N H A L A C I D E M T A N
A O C G Y G N I L T S U H E
T I R A A G N M O U F A S L
H T B P T I R A P R E E D T
G A O L Y E R E I M A E T S
I C R O I U R D L R E S S I
L U D M E S R E T L T T D R
N D R I O O T H R V A E E B
U E A N F N L E A N N P O A
S R I T F I I R R O B M Y T
E C N E N H A C I I R U R N
T T A G I C N T A S E R E E
A E G R S S U I S S V C L G
R R E A H A I N G U D T L A
I R M L C R H S A C A R A M
M A I S L A T H E R I N G P
E C L A I M E D D E V A R B
U E Z M U R T C E P S Z L E
```

Answer on page 124.

Just a Fantasy

BIGFOOT

BROWNIE

CHANGELING

CYCLOPS

DOPPELGÄNGER

DRAGON

DWARF

FAIRY

GNOME

GREMLIN

HOBBIT

HOBGOBLIN

LEPRECHAUN

LOCH NESS MONSTER

MARTIAN

MEDUSA

MERMAID

MINOTAUR

PEGASUS

PHOENIX

PIXIE

POLTERGEIST

SANDMAN

SPHINX

SPRITE

TROLL

UNICORN

VAMPIRE

WILL-O'-THE-WISP

```
N N W M I N O T A U R E M C
O E I A N T H E N K I N N H
G D L L O R T I R O A Y F A
A T R O B L C L E I T R W N
R E I N W O R B T H A I T G
D R F E R S G R S I L A D E
E I R N S U A B N L N F T L
D E A R U M G N O M E I D I
T A W M A A B T M H R O S N
O S D R R I H D S P P P A G
O U I G E E P C S P H I N X
F D N E W E M O E T T X D I
G E H I G E G L N R K I M N
I M S A I R G N H D P E A E
B P S T E A E H C O A E N O
T U S M N T A T O R B T L H
S S L G A R G U L M E B N P
T I E R I P M A V O S O I N
N R L I N C Y C L O P S E T
```

Answer on page 125.

Outer Space

ANDROMEDA

ANTARES

AQUARIUS

ASTEROID

BETELGEUSE

CALLISTO

CASSIOPEIA

COMET

CONSTELLATIONS

COSMIC DUST

DRACO

DWARF PLANET

GANYMEDE

GEMINI

LIBRA

MARS

MERCURY

METEOR SHOWER

NEPTUNE

ORION

PLUTO

PULSAR

RED GIANT

ROCKET SHIP

SATELLITE

SCORPIUS

SHOOTING STAR

SPACE STATION

VEGA

VENUS

```
M R A T S G N I T O O H S R
R E T E N U T P E N H E E U
O N R T N A I G D E R W I V
C E R C S N E R I G O S D A
K O P R U D E T A H T W Y A
E B N I G R P N S U A L R N
T A C S E O Y R I R Q B F O
S S I T T M O S F J I A U I
H U U S E E T P U L S A R T
I I U D T D L S E R A T N A
P P E E C A L L I S T O N T
S R M I N I T S A E E O G S
M O S E L V M T I T I K E E
E C T A N A E S E R I A M C
V S W U R L F N O M U O I A
E L W S L A S T U C O E N P
G O A I E P O I S S A C I S
A S T E R O I D R A C O F S
P E S U E G L E T E B A C E
```

Answer on page 125.

Dance Steps

BALLET

BALLROOM

BOLERO

BUNNY HOP

CANCAN

CHA-CHA

CHARLESTON

CLOG

CONGA LINE

CONTEMPORARY

DISCO

ELECTRIC SLIDE

FLAMENCO

HULA

HUSTLE

INTERPRETIVE

IRISH STEP

JITTERBUG

MACARENA

MERENGUE

MINUET

MODERN

MORRIS

POLKA

REEL

RUMBA

SALSA

TANGO

TURKEY TROT

TWIST

ZYDECO

```
R T E E A N E U G N E R E M
A E G B E S R S B O N D O T
E Z E O G I L A K T I R O E
N Y K L U A L A O L R R L A
I D E E B L G G S I I T L E
L E N R R E N C S R S U A C
A C V O E A I T I U H N O G
G O O I T R N E H W S N D A
N M N C T U R K E Y T R O T
O E S C I E A N T E E T W N
C H E E J R R A M T P I O E
N L M O F E N P F I S T V E
E E V A D A O E R T S R Y A
M D S O C R I A T E L L A B
A I M N A A K N L E T G L M
L S A R E L R R H O U N U U
F C Y R O O A E R S O N I R
W O E P O H Y N N U B A I S
S G O L C H A C H A U M E M
```

Answer on page 126.

Flower Garden

ACACIA

AMARYLLIS

AZALEA

BLACK-EYED SUSAN

CALLA LILY

CAMELLIA

CROCUS

DAHLIA

FOXGLOVE

GLADIOLA

GOLDENROD

HIBISCUS

HYDRANGEA

IMPATIENS

JASMINE

LAVENDER

LILAC

LOTUS

MARIGOLD

MORNING GLORY

OLEANDER

ORCHID

PERIWINKLE

PETUNIA

POINSETTIA

SNAPDRAGON

TULIP

ZINNIA

B M R A I T T E S N I O P O
N S A C P E T U N I A C O L
O N I R I I S S O I A F L N
G E L O I W E U R R M B A U
A I L T W G E T C D O S N T
R T E T H I O O H N U K A Y
D A M A R Y L L I S O U S J
P P A D O R N E D L O G H M
A M C O U H L E D R G I O V
N I E E A B Y O E U Q R U E
S T L A V E N D E R N O T F
U I T H K O N A R I S A U A
C L V C A A L A N A L E L C
S I A N E D A G Z I N N I A
I L T L I Z G N X E S G P C
B A O D A L S U C O R C E I
I C A L O I D A L G F A Y A
H P E R I W I N K L E P R E
S A Y L I L A L L A C E N T

Answer on page 126.

Yoga

ABHYASA

ANAHATA

ANANDA

ASHTANGA

BHAGAVAD GITA

BHAKTI

CHAKRAS

CORE STRENGTH

FOCUS

IYENGAR

KARMA

KUMBHAKA

KUNDALINI

MANIPURA

MANTRA

MULADHARA

NAMASTE

PRANAYAMA

RELAXING

RESTORATIVE

SAVASANA

SHANTI

SURYA NAMASKAR

SVADHISHTHANA

TANTRA

VAIRAGYA

VINYASA

VISHUDDHA

```
T H E R A R A H D A L U M E
S A R V I S H U D D H A E G
A M R A K I L V O N B A L S
R C M O M M N P I A E T U I
K T A G A I O I N N S R I S
A S N N N N W H L A Y I V C
H U I I T K A H B A H A Y O
C C P X R G V A N A D S S P
E O U A A S A A N H A N R A
V F R L K H M S I A R A U E
I P A E E A R S F R N R A K
T A O R S N H R M A A A B E
A D S K A T S B Y A C G H A
R O A H H I R A M M P N Y N
O R E A T T M E I U T E A A
T I N V E A S P N O K Y S H
S A V A S A N A R G T I A A
E T S A M A N G A R T N A T
R A T I G D A V A G A H B A
```

Answer on page 127.

Amusement Park

ARCADE

BUMPER CARS

CHURROS

DISNEY

FAIRGROUND

FESTIVAL

FRIES

FUNHOUSE

FUNNEL CAKE

GO-KARTS

HALL OF MIRRORS

HAYRIDE

HOT DOGS

KIDDIE RIDES

MERRY-GO-ROUND

MIDWAY

ORLANDO

PARADE

PETTING ZOO

POPCORN

ROLLER COASTER

SIX FLAGS

SKEE-BALL

SLIDE

SOFT PRETZELS

TICKETS

TILT-A-WHIRL

TRAIN

WATER PARK

```
I  B  D  N  U  O  R  G  R  I  A  F  H  S
M  E  F  U  N  H  O  U  S  E  L  O  I  R
E  E  S  T  E  K  C  I  T  V  T  E  O  A
T  O  R  L  A  N  D  O  H  D  A  L  T  C
S  R  O  R  R  I  M  F  O  L  L  A  H  R
A  I  T  N  Y  Y  P  G  A  E  R  V  A  E
K  S  X  W  H  G  S  E  R  S  R  I  Y  P
M  E  S  F  N  R  O  C  P  O  P  T  R  M
S  I  E  O  L  M  O  R  E  R  O  S  I  U
E  W  D  N  E  A  Z  T  O  R  E  E  D  B
K  A  I  W  S  L  G  L  S  U  Y  F  E  O
A  T  R  T  A  U  N  S  A  H  N  G  O  O
C  E  E  D  J  Y  I  A  R  C  A  D  E  S
L  R  I  H  W  A  T  L  I  T  O  K  L  E
E  P  D  E  I  S  T  A  N  A  R  I  D  I
N  A  D  I  S  N  E  Y  M  U  D  A  S  R
N  R  I  E  M  E  P  N  T  E  R  P  I  F
U  K  K  A  S  K  E  E  B  A  L  L  R  N
F  S  L  E  Z  T  E  R  P  T  F  O  S  K
```

Answer on page 127.

Zzzzzzzzzz

AZALEA

BLINTZ

BLIZZARD

BUZZWORD

CAPSIZE

CHEEZ WHIZ

CITIZEN

FUZZY-WUZZY

GAZPACHO

GLITZ

HAZELNUT

HUZZAH

JACUZZI

KLUTZ

MOZZARELLA

PAPARAZZI

PIZZAZZ

PIZZERIA

RAZZLE-DAZZLE

SCHMOOZE

SHOW BIZ

SNAZZY

SPRITZER

SWIZZLE STICK

WALTZ

ZANZIBAR

ZESTY

ZIGZAG

ZIMBABWE

ZODIAC

ZOMBIES

ZURICH

```
S  C  H  M  O  O  Z  E  Z  I  S  P  A  C
R  A  A  T  G  L  I  T  Z  H  T  H  E  Z
E  N  L  E  Z  O  O  A  O  I  D  O  L  T
Z  E  L  Z  T  L  A  W  Z  E  G  N  A  U
T  Z  E  S  R  A  B  I  Z  N  A  Z  Z  L
I  I  R  L  N  I  O  O  Z  Y  Z  E  A  K
R  T  A  I  Z  Z  A  R  A  P  A  P  C  G
P  I  Z  Z  A  Z  Z  B  R  A  S  I  P  H
S  C  Z  I  M  B  A  B  W  E  T  R  A  I
Y  Z  O  Z  H  E  C  D  O  S  Z  Z  Y  P
Z  K  M  Z  I  W  N  G  E  S  E  I  I  Z
Z  Z  Y  U  D  E  Z  L  D  L  L  Z  A  G
U  O  Z  C  Z  R  Z  E  N  B  Z  O  A  I  I
W  M  Z  A  Y  Z  A  U  E  E  S  Z  C  C
Y  B  A  J  I  F  T  Z  R  H  P  T  A  I
Z  I  N  W  O  R  Z  I  Z  A  C  N  I  R
Z  E  S  T  Y  O  A  N  C  I  K  I  D  U
U  S  H  A  Z  Z  U  H  I  N  L  L  O  Z
F  G  O  U  D  R  O  W  Z  Z  U  B  Z  T
```

Answer on page 128.

You Earned It

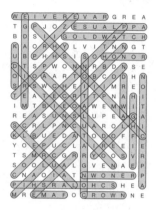

Great job solving this word search! We mean it, we're super proud of you! Let's go solve another one!

A Day at the Beach

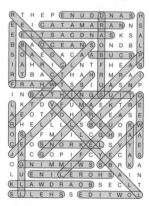

The pink sand beach in the Bahamas is pink due to the shells of microscopic coral insects.

Ice Cream Shop

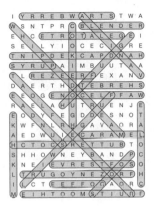

It wasn't precisely ice cream, but Alexander the Great enjoyed snow flavored with honey and nectar.

Knitting and Crafts

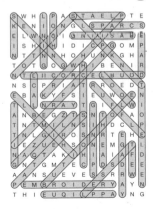

What English idiom thought to be inspired by sewing and clothesmaking means "everything"?

[The whole nine yards]

Under the Sea

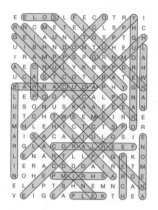

Electric eels can stun their prey, but they also use their electrical signal like radar to help them navigate.

Art Is Everywhere

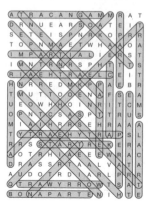

"A true artist is not one who is inspired but one who inspires others."—Salvador Dalí

Motown Hits

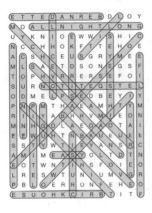

Do you know which of these great songs, performed by the Marvelettes, was Motown's first number one hit?

["Please, Mr. Postman"]

Let's Make a Movie

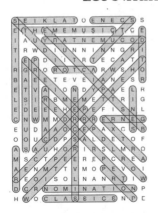

Oscar-winning director Steven Soderbergh filmed a couple of his most recent movies on an iPhone.

Speaking My Language

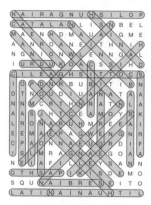

"Libel" and "mug" mean one thing in English, but in Dutch they mean "dragonfly" and "mosquito."

American Revolution

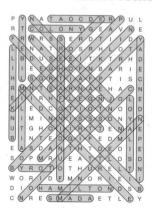

Paul Revere didn't shout "The British are coming!" (He needed to spread the word more discreetly.)

It's Greek to Me

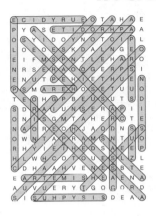

They say don't look a gift horse in the mouth, but during the Trojan War this would have been a very good idea.

Fly by Night (and also day)

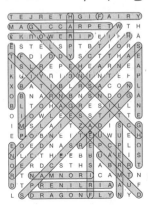

The fastest bird is the peregrine falcon and the slowest is a tie between all the birds that can't fly.

At the Library

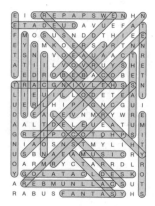

"I have found the most valuable thing in my wallet is my library card."
—Laura Bush

T for Two

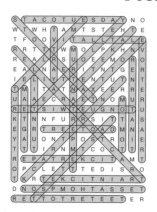

Now what's the "T for Two" phrase meaning "in utter confusion" or "in complete disorder"?

[Topsy-turvy]

110

Antique Store

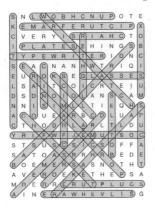

Not everything in an antique store is an antique, but "old stuff store" doesn't have the same ring.

On the Road

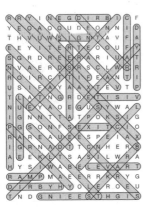

If you don't have your driver's license yet and you want to go for a spin, there's always a merry-go-round.

World Traveler

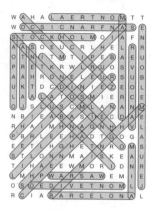

What two four-letter world cities can be scrambled together to make the word "memorial"?

[Lima and Rome.]

A Silly Puzzle

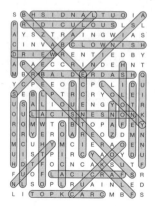

Silly String was invented by accident by people trying to produce a spray-on cast for sprained limbs.

Olympic Sports

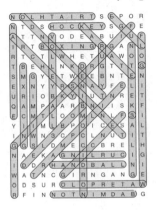

Sports set to debut at the twenty-twenty-four Paris Olympics include breakdancing and surfing.

Wide World of Color

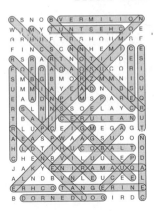

Snowy egrets, house finches, and common mynas also lay blue eggs, as do the blue jay and bluebird.

What's Your Hobby?

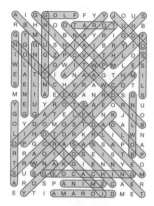

If your hobby is bowling, that means you enjoy making spares in your spare time.

Fun and Games

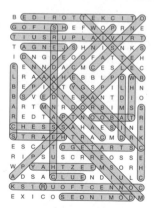

Before thinking of the name Scrabble, its inventor tried the names Criss Cross Words and Lexico.

Remember When

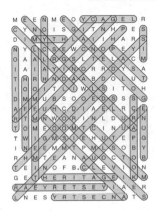

"Memory ... is the diary ... we all carry about with us."
—Oscar Wilde (in "The Importance of Being Earnest")

Feeling Good

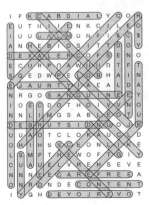

If you think cloud nine is too crowded, we hear good things about clouds one, two, five, seven, and eight.

On the Farm

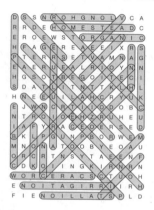

Scarecrows are extremely good at their job. They are known to be out standing in their field.

Bling

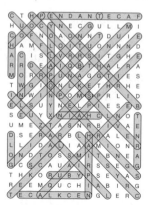

The Cullinan diamond is the largest in the world (unless you mean baseball diamonds, because those are much bigger).

Ten Spots

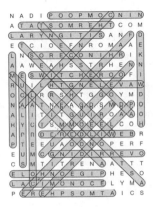

Nadia Comaneci of Romania was the first gymnast to score a perfect ten at the Olympics.

Red, Red, and More Red

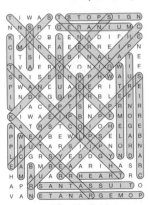

"I want to be different. If everyone is wearing black, I want to be wearing red."—Maria Sharapova

Wild West

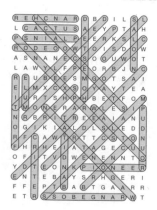

Billy the Kid was an outlaw for just six years before being killed at the age of twenty-one by Sheriff Pat Garrett.

Very Online

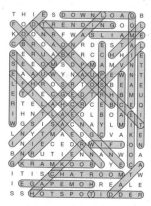

This book of word searches may not be technologically advanced, but in a way it is wireless.

Romantic Comedies

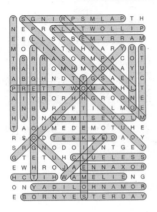

There's both a rom-com and a horror film named "Mother's Day," so don't get the wrong one.

Spa Day

A spa with someone on staff who is really great at massages could promote them as the Wizard of Aahs.

It's Showtime!

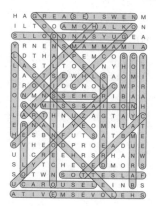

"Hamilton" earned the most Tony award nominations, but "The Producers" has the most wins.

Fine Arts

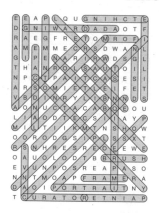

A quote from Edward Hopper: "If you could say it in words, there would be no reason to paint."

Back to School

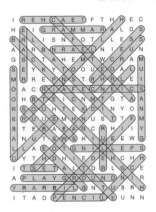

"If the child is not learning the way you are teaching, then you must teach in the way the child learns."—Rita Dunn

Music, Music, Music

A Grammy for Best Disco Song was given only once; it was won by Gloria Gaynor for "I Will Survive."

Quiet, Please

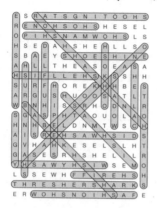

She sells seashells by the seashore ... but shouldn't she sell her shells elsewhere?

These Make Scents

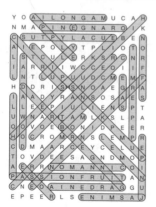

You can make potpourri with dried rose petals, lavender, rosemary, cloves, and orange peels.

Take Me to Your Leader

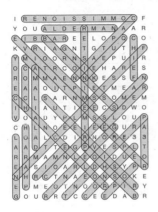

If you are looking to purchase some aromatic wood, you could instead say "Take me to your cedar."

Birdwatching

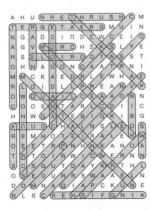

A hummingbird weighs less than a nickel, while an ostrich weighs more than twenty thousand nickels.

It's Wine O'Clock

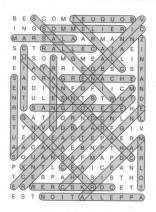

Becoming a master sommelier is so difficult that only five percent of applicants pass the test.

Anagram Pairs

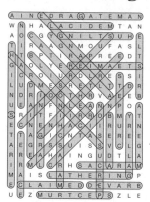

What anagram of "aspire" do you deserve for finishing this puzzle?

[Praise]

Just a Fantasy

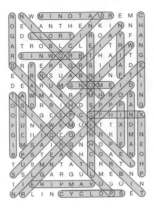

We mean the kind of troll that resides under a bridge, not the kind that starts arguments online.

[Though both are pretty awful.]

Outer Space

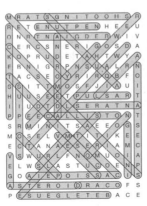

"The universe is a pretty big place. ... if it's just us, it seems like an awful waste of space." [from the film "Contact," based on the novel by Carl Sagan]

Dance Steps

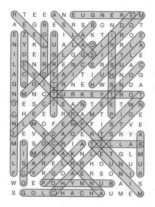

Teenagers on TikTok are generating new dances at the rate of five every single hour (or so we assume).

Flower Garden

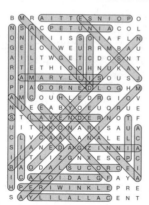

Broccoli is a flower, but we don't think you should give a bouquet of it as a Valentine's Day present.

Yoga

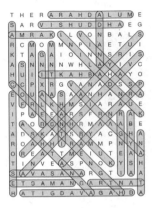

There are global competitions in which yoga asanas are performed as a competitive sport.

Amusement Park

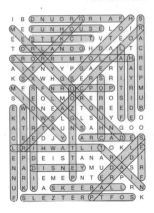

I believe that any park where someone tells you a good joke is an amusement park.

Zzzzzzzz

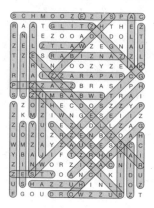

At the zoo, a dozen snoozy zebras prize cozy king-sized La-Z-Boys for zonking out.

About the Authors

ERIC AND JANINNE BERLIN previously created three other word search books for Union Square & Co. (Janinne worked behind the scenes, but is now a co-author.) They live in Connecticut with their dog and two children. Eric's word puzzles have appeared in newspapers and magazines nationwide, and are available online at puzzlesnacks.com. He also creates live puzzle events for kids and families at schools and museums. Eric and Janinne are both members of the National Puzzlers' League.